Monuments

by

Stephen Evans

For those who remember those who don't.

This is a work of fiction. The names, characters, places, and incidents are either the products of the author's imagination or are used fictitiously, and any resemblance to actual persons living or dead, business establishments, events, or locales is entirely coincidental.

For production permissions and rights, contact: info@istephenevans.com

"Dear son of memory, great heir of fame,
What need'st thou such weak witness of thy
name?"

John Milton.

STEPHEN EVANS

Contents

STEPHEN EVANS

Monuments
Original Version

STEPHEN EVANS

Cast of Characters

WALDO   Ralph Waldo Emerson, age 69

NELLY   Emerson's Daughter Ellen, age 33[1], referred to as Nelly in this play because the playwright was getting confused.

ELLEN   Emerson's first wife, Ellen, age 21[1]

Scene

A boat on the Nile River.

Time

1873.

---

[1] May be played by the same actress.

STEPHEN EVANS

ACT I SCENE 1

Setting: Emerson's cabin. Downstage right is a desk, chair behind, so the actor faces the audience. Up left is a doorway. Downstage from that is a window of sorts.

At Rise: WALDO is at his desk. He is struggling to light an oil lamp.

WALDO

Let there be light.

NELLY

From offstage

Papa, you should come out on deck. You can see the pyramids.

WALDO

I imagine they will last until the return trip.

Nelly enters.

NELLY

What are you working on, Papa?

> WALDO

Genesis.

She laughs.

> NELLY

Can you be more specific?

> WALDO

Chapter 1, verse 3.

He fiddles with the lamp.

> NELLY

Are you writing about it?

> WALDO

No, I am re-enacting it.

He fiddles some more, without success, then throws up his hands.

> WALDO

Let there be light!

She moves to the desk and lights the lamp for him.

> NELLY

There. Now you can call the light day.

WALDO

Squinting

I would call this dim not day.

NELLY

And set about dividing the darkness from the light.

WALDO

Wishful thinking, daughter.

NELLY

As you have always done, Papa.

She kisses his forehead and looks at the desk.

NELLY

What are you working on today instead of talking a stroll on deck with your devoted daughter?

WALDO

Plutarch's Morals. I wish Henry were here. He knew the Greeks so much better than I.

Ellen is struck with sadness, her brilliant father's decline brought home again, as it is many times each day.

NELLY

He is gone, Papa. Henry Thoreau died ten years ago.

Waldo stops, confused and then struggles to remember, accepts, then tries to cover his struggle. Nelly, ever the loving daughter, waits patiently for his mind to catch up.

WALDO
Then I change my mind. I don't wish he were here. He would be annoyed with me for disturbing his lecture to the Almighty.

Nelly laughs, but the sadness shows through.

NELLY
You are a wise man.

Waldo, all too aware of his decline, smiles.

WALDO
So everyone tells me.

NELLY
Do you doubt it, O Sage of Concord?

WALDO
Among many things.

Nelly tries to change the subject.

NELLY
I thought Plutarch was a Roman.

WALDO

No. He was a citizen of the Empire, but he was
Greek by birth, and by thought.

NELLY

Plutarch was one of my favorites as a child. When
you were away on your speaking tours, I would
sneak into your study and read him.

WALDO

You were a precocious child. I credit your mother
with that. I was away so often. Did you read the
Lives?

NELLY

No. Too stuffy, too many wars. I liked the Morals
actually. Is this Professor Goodwin's translation?

WALDO

Yes. Saved from the fire. I am to write the
introduction and must have it ready soon.

*Again, the sadness hits her. She gathers
herself, crosses back to the desk, and lays her
hand on his shoulder with great tenderness.*

NELLY

That is already done, Papa.

She turns to the front of the book.

NELLY

Reading

With an introduction by Ralph Waldo Emerson.

*Waldo looks at the book, confused. He turns a
few pages. Then turns a few back, always the
familiar struggle to comprehend, catch up
with the world.*

WALDO

It is done.

Another pause.

Wonderful!

He relaxes.

Oh I am quite relieved. I was dreading the labor.
The words do not flow as easily these days.

*He shakes it off, returning to a
familiar quotation to explain the
lapse.*

But who cares? As soon as we walk out of doors,
Nature transcends all poets so far, that a little more
or less skill in whistling is of no account.[2]

*Nelly understands, glances outside, then at
him, and takes charge, as she has so often
done and will continue to do for the rest of his*

---

[2] From a letter to Caroline Sturgis, Oct. 23, 1857

life.

NELLY
Papa, come out of this stuffy cabin and we'll find chairs in the sun and watch the ages float past us.

He smiles at her, grateful for her concern and her care.

The smile fades.

He looks around the cabin, again deep in confusion.

WALDO
This is a boat.

NELLY
Yes, Papa.

Waldo tries to solve the puzzle.

WALDO
Not on the ocean.

NELLY
No.

WALDO
A river?

NELLY

Yes.

WALDO

A river.

NELLY

Yes.

He looks out the window.

WALDO

The Concord?

NELLY

No.

WALDO

No. Too large. Nor the Charles either.

NELLY

It is the Nile.

Pause.

WALDO

The Nile?

NELLY

We are in Egypt, Papa. We are sailing down the Nile on a boat named the Aurora. Remember how shocked we were at the price? Eight dollars a day.

Slowly it dawns and he catches up.

WALDO
Yes. I remember now. Can we afford such extravagance?

She puts a hand on his shoulder.

NELLY
We can. Remember the fire?

WALDO
The fire. Yes! The fire.

NELLY
The fire burned our house.

WALDO
Yes. Yes. Our poor home.

NELLY
Then your friends and so many admirers raised the money to send us on this trip while it is restored.

He is lost in thought for a moment. Then he notices the book in front of him and turns back to it, something solid he understands.

WALDO
According to Plutarch, the Egyptians invented horticulture.

NELLY

And slavery.

WALDO

The Egyptians did not invent slavery. They merely perfected it.

NELLY

That I thought was an American accomplishment.

WALDO

Now, now. Mr. Lincoln fixed all that.

NELLY[3]

Papa, surely you don't think--

She sees him smiling.

Yes, you know me well.

Nelly picks up the volume, flips through.

NELLY

I loved these stories. Especially...

She finds the one she wants

Isis and Osiris. I used to read this one over and over.

---

[3] Ellen, her mother Lidian, Henry Thoreau, and about half of Concord were staunch abolitionists and initially supporters of John Brown. Emerson, though not as personally passionate, sometimes lent his famous name to the cause.

WALDO
That is hardly a story for children!

NELLY[4]
Exactly why I loved it! It is the oldest love story in the world. Osiris was entombed by Typhon and thrown into the sea and Isis searched all over the world for him and opened the coffin and took out the body and laid her cheek against his and then Typhon found the body and cut it up into pieces and threw it into the Nile and Isis searched the river and found every piece except—

WALDO
Yes. Yes. I know the story.

NELLY
For a young girl, it was scandalous. And very romantic.

Waldo gazes out the window.

WALDO
It happened here, if it happened. Thousands of years ago. The tomb of Osiris is on the island of—

---

[4] Ellen never married, living in her father's house for the rest of her life, an adoring aunt to her sibling's children.

> NELLY

Philae[5].

> WALDO

Philae, which lies...

> NELLY

Not far ahead of us.

*Philae reminds Waldo of something. He starts
to drift away into memory.*

> WALDO

I have wanted to see Philae for many years.

> NELLY

The captain tells me that the Wards are there, with
Clover Adams[6].

> WALDO

Many many years.

> NELLY

I arranged transportation for us on Philae so we
may join them straightaway.

*He pauses, then comes back. He turns to
Nelly, takes her hands, and looks at her*

---

[5] Pronounced Fi-Lee
[6] Wife of Henry Adams and the inspiration for some of
Henry James characters.

approvingly.

WALDO

You remind me of your mother, Ellen.

*She brushes the white hair away from his
forehead.*

NELLY

I was named for her, Papa. But your first wife Ellen
was not my mother.

He laughs.

WALDO

I am forgetful now I know. But that I have not
forgotten. Your mother Lidian is the best woman,
the best wife. She deserves...she deserves...you.
You should be home helping her restore our home,
not running away to foreign lands with your old
Papa.

Waldo stares at his hands.

NELLY

Don't think of that now. There will be time enough
for setting things right when we return home. If
mother and Edith have not already done so.

WALDO

If anyone can, it is...Lidian. She is...the best woman, the best wife.

NELLY

Papa?

WALDO

Yes?

NELLY

I often wonder...

WALDO

As do I. In the blood I suppose. The wandering wondering Emersons.

NELLY

I often wonder, I was saying.

WALDO

If you are saying, you might as well say.

NELLY

I often wonder how you managed to convince Mother to name me after your first wife. And not just one name. She was Ellen Tucker Emerson. I am Ellen Tucker Emerson.

WALDO

You have wondered that?

NELLY

Can you blame me?

WALDO

I suppose not. Best ask your mother.

NELLY

I have. She said to ask you.

WALDO

Did she?

NELLY

She did. I think she was curious what your answer
would be.

WALDO

So am I.

NELLY

I would like to know. If you remember.

WALDO

While I remember, you mean.

NELLY

You must have been quite persuasive. Even for
Ralph Waldo Emerson.

WALDO

I suppose it was my idea. Back then I had that
much audacity, and that little understanding of
women. But your mother agreed.

NELLY
Apparently. But why?

WALDO
My first wife and I were married not even two years before she died, and she was ill with the consumption so much of that. I think we knew before we married.

NELLY
Knew what?

WALDO
That we had not much time.

He is lost in thought again. Then, again, returns to the book.

WALDO
I wish Henry were here. He knew the Greeks so much better than I.

Nelly sighs.

NELLY
I shall be on deck, Papa, riddling the sphinx. Join me.

Nelly exits.

WALDO
One monument to another, eh?

He continues to turn pages, then finally finds what he wants.

WALDO

Reading

With an introduction by Ralph Waldo Emerson.

He turns a few pages.

WALDO

Reading

Plutarch's popularity will return in rapid cycles. If over-read in this decade, so that his anecdotes and opinions become commonplace, and to-day's novelties are sought for variety, his sterling values will presently recall the eye and thought of the best minds, and his books will be reprinted and read anew by coming generations. And thus Plutarch will be perpetually rediscovered from time to time as long as books last.[7]

He closes the book.

---

[7] *Plutarch's Morals, with an Introduction by Ralph Waldo Emerson*

Waldo

It is finished. I didn't know. I didn't remember. But how can one know what has been forgotten? Is there some sign? An empty space where memories used to be? Like a piece missing from a puzzle? I would like to know what I don't know. Even if that is the only thing I can know.

He opens the book again, turns the pages more and more rapidly, almost desperately, then finally finds what he wants.

Waldo
Reading

And in the first place where she could take rest, and found herself to be now at liberty and alone, she opened the ark, and laid her cheeks upon the cheeks of Osiris, and embraced him and wept bitterly[8].

Ellen O.S.

We knew.

This voice. He can almost remember it.

Waldo

We knew?

---

[8] *Of Isis and Osiris*, Plutarch's Morals

ELLEN O.S.
That we had not much time.

More familiar.

WALDO
Did we?

ELLEN O.S.
We spoke of it.

Waldo closes the book. He knows, but cannot believe.

WALDO
I do not believe in the immortality of the individual soul.

ELLEN O.S.
Since when?

He stands. The light grows around him.

WALDO
Since I lost you.

He turns upstage. Ellen is revealed upstage, wearing her funeral dress. Her face is covered by a veil.

ELLEN
You never lost me.

> WALDO
>
> I couldn't find you.

> ELLEN
>
> It's not the same.

> WALDO
>
> Nothing is.

> ELLEN
>
> Nothing is.

Ellen crosses down into the light.

> ELLEN
>
> Anyway I'm not a ghost or a spirit or a lost soul. I'm a memory.

> WALDO
>
> Well then I suppose you can stay. There is plenty of room. Most of the other memories have left. And they took yesterday with them.

> ELLEN
>
> You haven't forgotten me, have you, Waldo? Have you forgotten your Ellinelli? Your Lady Frolick? Lady Pensero? Have you forgotten your queen, my king?

> WALDO
>
> Facts fade. Feelings remain.

ELLEN

You can't have forgotten everything. Else I would
not be here.

WALDO

How can one know?

ELLEN

A puzzle. But then you like puzzles.

WALDO

Do I?

ELLEN

I hope so. I am one.

She laughs. He smiles at the sound.

WALDO

That is familiar.

ELLEN

Shall I remind you?

WALDO

Yes. Remind me. Please. Re<u>mind</u> me.

ELLEN

We met on Christmas day. You were my favorite
gift. I was a woman of 16 and you were a boy of 24.
We spoke of Byron. You thought I meant the poet
and I thought you meant my spaniel. We were very
confused for a moment, and then then your stern
and serious ministerial face crinkled up and you
laughed and laughed. And I decided then and there
that you would marry me.

WALDO

You had a dog named Byron. I thought that was
funny.

ELLEN

That you remember! I would be insulted but he
was a very good dog.

WALDO

Byron.

ELLEN

A year later you brought me a book called *Forget
Me Not*. A year! Now that is funny.

WALDO

That is ironic. It's not the same.

ELLEN

What is ironic is that I grew up in Concord, New
Hampshire, and after I died you settled in
Concord, Massachusetts.

WALDO

That is not ironic. It is a coincidence, and possibly
a metaphor.

ELLEN

I wanted to be a poet and you wanted to be a
minister. You ended up a poet and I ended up a
memory. What is that?

WALDO

That is a tragedy.

ELLEN

Oh, your poetry is not that bad.

He looks at her.

WALDO

That is funny.

She curtseys.

ELLEN

Are they coming back?

WALDO

What?

ELLEN
The memories.

WALDO
Oh they come back occasionally. They just don't
stay. Memories are like some old aunt who goes in
and out of the house, and occasionally recites
anecdotes of old times and persons which I
recognize as having heard before, and she being
gone again I search in vain for any trace.[9]

ELLEN
That sounds like something you wrote.

WALDO
I don't recall.

ELLEN
Shall I?

WALDO
What?

ELLEN
Stay?

He looks offstage where Nelly has exited.

WALDO
Ellen is...out there.

---

[9] *Essay on Memory*, Emerson

ELLEN

I am Ellen.

WALDO

You are Ellinelli. You are Lady Frolick and Lady Pensero.

ELLEN

I believe so.

WALDO

I have remembered something that I have forgotten.

ELLEN

You had forgotten but now you remember?

WALDO

No, I remember that I have forgotten.

ELLEN

I see.

WALDO

I have tried and tried.

ELLEN

Yes?

WALDO

For some time, I have tried.

ELLEN

Yes?

WALDO

I cannot recall.

ELLEN

Say it.

WALDO

Your face. I cannot recall your face.

ELLEN

Is that all?

WALDO

I want to. Very much. But I cannot.

ELLEN

I'm almost glad. I was not so beautiful toward the end. So pale and thin.

WALDO

You were always beautiful.

ELLEN

But wait. You have my miniature still?

WALDO

Your picture. Yes. I have it in my study. Or I did. Who knows where it is now? I don't think it burned. Though that night was so confusing.

ELLEN

Poor Waldo.

WALDO

That I remember. You called me that often.

ELLEN

If you have the miniature, then you can't have
forgotten how I looked.

WALDO

I look at the painting. Often. But I do not recognize
you when I see it.

ELLEN

Was it not a good likeness?

WALDO

It's not that. It just doesn't feel the same.

ELLEN

The same?

WALDO

As when I looked at you. I still remember the way I
felt. Transcendent.

ELLEN

Transcendent? You make me sound very grand.

WALDO

You were.

ELLEN

Transcendent? No. I was a girl in love, for the first and only time. You mistake transcendent for incandescent.

Her lighting brightens a bit

WALDO

Transcendent sounds better.

ELLEN

You're just used to it[10].

WALDO

Perhaps.

ELLEN

I suppose I was a little transcendent, towards the end. It was so hard to hold on to life. I tried, for you.

WALDO

You were brave. I remember that.

ELLEN

We had so little time. I didn't want to waste it in tears.

---

[10] Emerson was the 'founder' of American Transcendentalism.

WALDO

And your cough. Your terrible cough. And the
blood. So much blood from such a tiny body.

ELLEN

I am healed now.

WALDO

I took you south, to try the climate.

ELLEN

To Philadelphia!

WALDO

And I had to leave you there and return to Boston.
I have never felt so alone.

ELLEN

I was the one in Philadelphia.

WALDO

And I was desperate to know if you missed me as
much as I missed you.

ELLEN

That is natural. You were so young.

WALDO

Natural. You were young. Was I ever young?

ELLEN

You were. You just didn't know it.

WALDO

I feel younger now, with you here.

ELLEN

Dear Waldo.

WALDO

Dear Waldo. I remember that, now, too. No one
else has ever called me that. Lidian calls me Mr.
Emerson. May I speak of her to you?

ELLEN

Sweet Waldo.

WALDO

I know she has never called me that. Not in my
hearing anyway.

ELLEN

You love her.

WALDO

It is, imprecise, to use the same word for what I felt
for you, and what I feel for her. But it is the only
word we are given. Even Shakespeare never found
another. So I suppose we must make do.

ELLEN

But this dream of love, though beautiful, is only
one scene in our play. In the procession of the soul
from within outward, it enlarges its circles ever,
like the pebble thrown into the pond, or the light
proceeding from an orb.[11]

WALDO

That sounds like something I once wrote.

ELLEN

It is.

WALDO

If you are a memory, how is it that you know
something I wrote years after.

ELLEN

Memories don't abide alone. We coexist.

WALDO

Really?

ELLEN

Oh yes. We speak to one another often.

WALDO

Memories speak to memories.

---

[11] *Essay on Love*, Emerson

ELLEN

Well, think of it. What else is there to do but speak
to each other? Especially when you spend so little
time with us. Such a busy important man, always
running around giving speeches.

WALDO

Lectures, not speeches. Politicians give speeches.

*She sticks her tongue out at him through the
veil, laughs, spinning away, her white dress
flowing around her. She stops, then turns slyly
back to Waldo.*

ELLEN

In fact, Lidian and I have spoken.

WALDO

Pardon?

ELLEN

Lidian. Your second wife. You member her, don't
you?

WALDO

Oh yes.

ELLEN

I thought so. Lidian and I have had long
conversations.

WALDO

About me?

ELLEN

Oh yes!

WALDO

Oh no.

ELLEN

And she does also call you poor Mr. Emerson, if
that is any consolation.

WALDO

For a memory, you are very chatty.

ELLEN

Memories are not miniatures.

WALDO

What are they? I don't remember.

ELLEN

Memory is a presumption of a possession of the
future. Now we are halves, we see the past but not
the future, but in that day will the hemisphere
complete itself and foresight be as perfect as
aftersight.[12]

---

[12] *Essay on Memory*, Emerson

WALDO

Or as imperfect. Did I write that?

ELLEN

Of course.

WALDO

It is like your face. Though I know it, I don't recognize it.

ELLEN

I like that one especially. It reminds me of your sermons. One of the saddest parts of being sick was that I could not attend your sermons.

WALDO

It reminds you?

ELLEN

You were so grand in the pulpit with your high cloak and sweet voice. And only once per sermon would you let yourself sneak a glance at your Ellinelli. And when you did look on my face, only for a second and with no smile or nod or sign, I knew I needed no other communion.

WALDO

Nor I.

He turns suddenly.

WALDO

I remember!

Ellen turns away.

ELLEN

My face?

WALDO

For a year afterwards, I walked each day to your grave.

He turns to her.

ELLEN

Poor Waldo.

WALDO

You asked me to.

ELLEN

Did I?

WALDO

Breathe not yet, but wait until
My spirit is set free.
Then whisper round my grave
The tale of my release —[13]

---

[13] *To the South Wind*, Ellen Emerson

ELLEN
I wrote that.

WALDO
You did.

ELLEN
And you remember.

WALDO
I do.

ELLEN
But you cannot recall my face.

WALDO
No. I remember I walked each day to your grave.

He takes a step toward her.

WALDO
I needed to see your face. Once more.

Another step. Dimmer.

WALDO
Just once more.

Another step, and he is near her.

WALDO
One day I entered your tomb.

She turns to him.

WALDO
And opened the coffin.

He reaches up to her veil.

WALDO
And I saw.

Her light goes out. He lowers his arm.

WALDO
Nothing.

ELLEN
Nothing?

WALDO
Nothing.

ELLEN
It was empty?

WALDO
We were in darkness.

ELLEN
That is natural.

WALDO
Natural. Yes. Does it bother you?

ELLEN

What?

WALDO

That I, came to see you?

ELLEN

I often come to see you.

WALDO

Are you sure you are not a ghost?

ELLEN

Maybe a memory is a ghost that lives inside us.

WALDO

Maybe a ghost is a memory that lives outside us.

ELLEN

But you don't believe in the immortality of the soul.

WALDO

Maybe that is where memories go. The afterlife belongs not to us but to them.

She steps into the light again.

ELLEN

Perhaps they are us.

WALDO

After you died, I resigned from the ministry. Your inheritance paid for long trip through Europe. I was lost, so I thought I may as well be lost somewhere new.

ELLEN

Clever Waldo.

WALDO

That's a new one. I wandered for a year. Syracuse. Naples. Rome. Florence. Paris. London.

ELLEN

So far from home.

WALDO

Without you I had no home.

ELLEN

So far then.

WALDO

I met great writers that I had admired: Landor, Coleridge, Wordsworth, Carlyle.

ELLEN

Your Heroes.

WALDO

I found them to be...just men. Poor men. Flawed men.

ELLEN

You were disappointed.

WALDO

Yes. But. It is a kind of freedom, to learn what is possible, and by whom.

ELLEN

It is.

WALDO

By the end I knew something in me had changed, but I did not know what.

ELLEN

I know.

WALDO

I came back, to Concord. I could not return to Boston and the church.

ELLEN

I understand.

WALDO

I had to make a living, so I started writing, and speaking.

She smiles.

ELLEN

Lecturing.

And he smiles.

WALDO
Lecturing. I married Lidian.

ELLEN
A good woman.

WALDO
A good woman.

ELLEN
You needed her.

WALDO
I loved her. Love her. You can tell her I said so.

ELLEN
You can tell her.

WALDO
I can tell her.

ELLEN
She gave you children.

WALDO
Ellen. Edith. Edward. Poor Waldo, gone so young.[14]

ELLEN
Poor Waldo. So much tragedy.

---

[14] Emerson's son Waldo died of scarlet fever at age five.

WALDO
So much life.

ELLEN
If I had not gotten sick...

WALDO
I could not have left you.

ELLEN
Maybe that is why I had to leave you.

WALDO
Let us build altars to the Beautiful Necessity.[15]

ELLEN
Though thou loved her as thyself,
As a self of purer clay,
Though her parting dims the day,
Stealing grace from all alive; [16]

WALDO
Heartily know,
When half-gods go,
The gods arrive. [17]

ELLEN
It's all right.

---

[15] *Essay on Experience*, Emerson
[16] *Give All to Love*, poem, Emerson

WALDO

I remember.

ELLEN

The loving. And the leaving. It is all right.

WALDO

Silent rushes the swift Lord
Through ruined systems still restored,
Broad-sowing, bleak and void to bless,
Plants with worlds the wilderness,
Waters with tears of ancient sorrow
Apples of Eden ripe to-morrow;
House and tenant go to ground.[17]

ELLEN

Lost in God.[18]

WALDO

In Godhead found.[18]

He returns to the desk.

WALDO

I have wondered from time to time what my last
memory will be. After all the others have escaped
me. What will be the last? Like Pandora's box, my
mind will shut tight, yet one will tap on the lid and
cry out 'wait! I am still here.'

---

[17] *Threnody*, poem, Emerson

He looks to Ellen.

WALDO

Will it be you? Lidian? Nelly? Henry? Little Waldo feverish in the bed? What will it be? What part of myself will be the last to say goodbye?

ELLEN

It may be a bit selfish but I should like it to be me. But it won't be.

She starts to exit.

ELLEN

It won't be me. Or Lidian. Or Nelly. Or Henry. Or little Waldo. For you it will be a boat on river in a land where history waits.

WALDO

I have lived two lives. One of the mind. One of the heart. The mind is leaving. Only the heart remains.

She turns back to him. He looks at her.

WALDO

One monument to another.

The light slowly fades.

THE END

Monuments
Extended Version

STEPHEN EVANS

Cast of Characters

WALDO   Ralph Waldo Emerson, age 69

NELLY   Emerson's Daughter Ellen, age 33, referred to as Nelly in this play because the playwright was getting confused.

ELLEN   Emerson's first wife, Ellen, age 21

HENRY   Henry Thoreau

Scene

A boat on the Nile River.

Time

1873.

STEPHEN EVANS

ACT I SCENE 1

Setting: Emerson's cabin. Downstage right is a desk, chair behind, so the actor faces the audience. Up left is a doorway. Downstage from that is a window of sorts.

At Rise: WALDO is at his desk. He is struggling to light an oil lamp.

WALDO

Let there be light.

NELLY

From offstage

Papa, you should come out on deck. You can see the pyramids.

WALDO

I imagine they will last until the return trip.

Nelly enters.

NELLY

What are you working on, Papa?

WALDO

Genesis.

She laughs.

NELLY
Can you be more specific?

WALDO
Chapter 1, verse 3.

He fiddles with the lamp.

NELLY
Are you writing about it?

WALDO
No, I am re-enacting it.

*He fiddles some more, without success,
then throws up his hands.*

WALDO
Let there be light!

*She moves to the desk and lights the lamp
for him.*

NELLY
There. Now you can call the light day.

WALDO
Squinting
I would call this dim not day.

NELLY

And set about dividing the darkness from the light.

WALDO

Wishful thinking, daughter.

NELLY

As you have always done, Papa.

She kisses his forehead and looks at the desk.

NELLY

What are you working on today instead of talking a stroll on deck with your devoted daughter?

WALDO

Plutarch's Morals. I wish Henry were here. He knew the Greeks so much better than I.

Ellen is struck with sadness, her brilliant father's decline brought home again, as it is many times each day.

NELLY

He is gone, Papa. Henry Thoreau died ten years ago.

Waldo stops, confused and then struggles to remember, accepts, then tries to cover his struggle. Nelly, ever the loving

*daughter, waits patiently for his mind to
catch up.*

WALDO

Then I change my mind. I don't wish he were
here. He would be annoyed with me for
disturbing his lecture to the Almighty.

*Nelly laughs, but the sadness shows
through.*

NELLY

You are a wise man.

*Waldo, all too aware of his decline,
smiles.*

WALDO

So everyone tells me.

NELLY

Do you doubt it, O Sage of Concord?

WALDO

Among many things.

Nelly tries to change the subject.

NELLY

I thought Plutarch was a Roman.

WALDO

No. He was a citizen of the Empire, but he was
Greek by birth, and by thought.

NELLY

Plutarch was one of my favorites as a child.
When you were away on your speaking tours,
I would sneak into your study and read him.

WALDO

You were a precocious child. I credit your
mother with that. I was away so often. Did you
read the Lives?

NELLY

No. Too stuffy, too many wars. I liked the
Morals actually. Is this Professor Goodwin's
translation?

WALDO

Yes. Saved from the fire. I am to write the
introduction and must have it ready soon.

*Again, the sadness hits her. She gathers
herself, crosses back to the desk, and lays
her hand on his shoulder with great
tenderness.*

NELLY

That is already done, Papa.

She turns to the front of the book.

NELLY

Reading

With an introduction by Ralph Waldo
Emerson.

> *Waldo looks at the book, confused. He*
> *turns a few pages. Then turns a few back,*
> *always the familiar struggle to*
> *comprehend, catch up with the world.*

WALDO

It is done.

> *Another pause.*

Wonderful!

> *He relaxes.*

Oh I am quite relieved. I was dreading the
labor. The words do not flow as easily these
days.

> *He shakes it off, returning to*
> *a familiar quotation to*
> *explain the lapse.*

But who cares? As soon as we walk out of
doors, Nature transcends all poets so far, that a
little more or less skill in whistling is of no
account.[18]

> *Nelly understands, glances outside, then*
> *at him, and takes charge, as she has so*

---

[18] From a letter to Caroline Sturgis, Oct. 23, 1857

*often done and will continue to do for the
rest of his life.*

NELLY

Papa, come out of this stuffy cabin and we'll
find chairs in the sun and watch the ages float
past us.

*He smiles at her, grateful for her concern
and her care.*

The smile fades.

*He looks around the cabin, again deep in
confusion.*

WALDO

This is a boat.

NELLY

Yes, Papa.

Waldo tries to solve the puzzle.

WALDO

Not on the ocean.

NELLY

No.

WALDO

A river?

                    NELLY
Yes.

                    WALDO
A river.

                    NELLY
Yes.

   He looks out the window.

                    WALDO
The Concord?

                    NELLY
No.

                    WALDO
No. Too large. Nor the Charles either.

                    NELLY
It is the Nile.

   Pause.

                    WALDO
The Nile?

                    NELLY
We are in Egypt, Papa. We are sailing down
the Nile on a boat named the Aurora.
Remember how shocked we were at the price?
Eight dollars a day.

Slowly it dawns and he catches up.

WALDO

Yes. I remember now. Can we afford such
extravagance?

She puts a hand on his shoulder.

NELLY

We can. Remember the fire?

WALDO

The fire. Yes! The fire.

NELLY

The fire burned our house.

WALDO

Yes. Yes. Our poor home.

NELLY

Then your friends and so many admirers
raised the money to send us on this trip while
it is restored.

*He is lost in thought for a moment. Then
he notices the book in front of him and
turns back to it, something solid he
understands.*

WALDO

According to Plutarch, the Egyptians invented
horticulture.

NELLY
And slavery.

WALDO
The Egyptians did not invent slavery. They merely perfected it.

NELLY
That I thought was an American accomplishment.

WALDO
Now, now. Mr. Lincoln fixed all that.

NELLY[19]
Papa, surely you don't think--

She sees him smiling.
Yes, you know me well.

Nelly picks up the volume, flips through.

NELLY
I loved these stories. Especially...

She finds the one she wants
Isis and Osiris. I used to read this one over and over.

---

[19] Ellen, her mother Lidian, Henry Thoreau, and about half of Concord were staunch abolitionists and initially supporters of John Brown. Emerson, though not as personally passionate, sometimes lent his famous name to the cause.

WALDO

That is hardly a story for children!

NELLY[20]

Exactly why I loved it! It is the oldest love story in the world. Osiris was entombed by Typhon and thrown into the sea and Isis searched all over the world for him and opened the coffin and took out the body and laid her cheek against his and then Typhon found the body and cut it up into pieces and threw it into the Nile and Isis searched the river and found every piece except—

WALDO

Yes. Yes. I know the story.

NELLY

For a young girl, it was scandalous. And very romantic.

Waldo gazes out the window.

WALDO

It happened here, if it happened. Thousands of years ago. The tomb of Osiris is on the island of—

---

[20] Ellen never married, living in her father's house for the rest of her life, an adoring aunt to her sibling's children.

NELLY

Philae[21].

WALDO

Philae, which lies...

NELLY

Not far ahead of us.

Philae reminds Waldo of something. He starts to drift away into memory.

WALDO

I have wanted to see Philae for many years.

NELLY

The captain tells me that the Wards are there, with Clover Adams[22].

WALDO

Many many years.

NELLY

I arranged transportation for us on Philae so we may join them straightaway.

He pauses, then comes back. He turns to Nelly, takes her hands, and looks at her approvingly.

---

[21] Pronounced Fi-Lee
[22] Wife of Henry Adams and the inspiration for some of Henry James characters.

WALDO

You remind me of your mother, Ellen.

She brushes the white hair away from his forehead.

NELLY

I was named for her, Papa. But your first wife Ellen was not my mother.

He laughs.

WALDO

I am forgetful now I know. But that I have not forgotten. Your mother Lidian is the best woman, the best wife. She deserves...she deserves...you. You should be home helping her restore our home, not running away to foreign lands with your old Papa.

Waldo stares at his hands.

NELLY

Don't think of that now. There will be time enough for setting things right when we return home. If mother and Edith have not already done so.

WALDO

If anyone can, it is...Lidian. She is...the best woman, the best wife.

NELLY

Papa?

WALDO

Yes?

NELLY

I often wonder...

WALDO

As do I. In the blood I suppose. The wandering wondering Emersons.

NELLY

I often wonder, I was saying.

WALDO

If you are saying, you might as well say.

NELLY

I often wonder how you managed to convince Mother to name me after your first wife. And not just one name. She was Ellen Tucker Emerson. I am Ellen Tucker Emerson.

WALDO

You have wondered that?

NELLY

Can you blame me?

WALDO

I suppose not. Best ask your mother.

NELLY

I have. She said to ask you.

WALDO

Did she?

NELLY

She did. I think she was curious what your
answer would be.

WALDO

So am I.

NELLY

I would like to know. If you remember.

WALDO

While I remember, you mean.

NELLY

You must have been quite persuasive. Even for
Ralph Waldo Emerson.

WALDO

I suppose it was my idea. Back then I had that
much audacity, and that little understanding of
women. But your mother agreed.

NELLY

Apparently. But why?

WALDO

My first wife and I were married not even two years before she died, and she was ill with the consumption so much of that. I think we knew before we married.

NELLY

Knew what?

WALDO

That we had not much time.

He is lost in thought again. Then, again, returns to the book.

WALDO

I wish Henry were here. He knew the Greeks so much better than I.

Nelly sighs.

NELLY

I shall be on deck, Papa, riddling the sphinx. Join me.

Nelly exits.

WALDO

One monument to another, eh?

He continues to turn pages, then finally finds what he wants.

WALDO

Reading

With an introduction by Ralph Waldo
Emerson.

He turns a few pages.

WALDO

Reading

Plutarch's popularity will return in rapid
cycles. If over-read in this decade, so that his
anecdotes and opinions become
commonplace, and to-day's novelties are
sought for variety, his sterling values will
presently recall the eye and thought of the
best minds, and his books will be reprinted
and read anew by coming generations. And
thus Plutarch will be perpetually rediscovered
from time to time as long as books last.[23]

He closes the book.

WALDO

It is finished. I didn't know. I didn't remember.
But how can one know what has been
forgotten? Is there some sign? An empty space
where memories used to be? Like a piece
missing from a puzzle? I would like to know

---

[23] *Plutarch's Morals, with an Introduction by Ralph
Waldo Emerson*

what I don't know. Even if that is the only thing I can know.

He opens the book again, turns the pages more and more rapidly, almost desperately, then finally finds what he wants.

WALDO

Reading

And in the first place where she could take rest, and found herself to be now at liberty and alone, she opened the ark, and laid her cheeks upon the cheeks of Osiris, and embraced him and wept bitterly[24].

ELLEN O.S.

We knew.

This voice. He can almost remember it.

WALDO

We knew?

ELLEN O.S.

That we had not much time.

More familiar.

---

[24] *Of Isis and Osiris*, Plutarch's Morals

WALDO

Did we?

ELLEN O.S.

We spoke of it.

*Waldo closes the book. He knows, but
cannot believe.*

WALDO

I do not believe in the immortality of the
individual soul.

ELLEN O.S.

Since when?

He stands. The light grows around him.

WALDO

Since I lost you.

*He turns upstage. Ellen is revealed
upstage, wearing her funeral dress. Her
face is covered by a veil.*

ELLEN

You never lost me.

WALDO

I couldn't find you.

ELLEN

It's not the same.

WALDO

Nothing is.

ELLEN

Nothing is.

Ellen crosses down into the light.

ELLEN

Anyway I'm not a ghost or a spirit or a lost soul. I'm a memory.

WALDO

Well then I suppose you can stay. There is plenty of room. Most of the other memories have left. And they took yesterday with them. Memories are like some old aunt who goes in and out of the house, and occasionally recites anecdotes of old times and persons which I recognize as having heard before, and she being gone again I search in vain for any trace.[25]

Waldo pauses, trying to remember.

WALDO

That sounds like something I once wrote.

ELLEN

It is.

---

[25] *Essay on Memory*, Emerson

WALDO

If you are a memory, how is it that you know
something I wrote years later.

ELLEN

Memories don't abide alone. We coexist.

WALDO

Really?

ELLEN

Oh yes. We even speak to one another.

WALDO

Speak?

HENRY

Let there be light.

*Waldo turns. Light comes up on Henry at
the desk. He is lighting the lamp.*

WALDO

Good morning Henry. How are the beans?

HENRY

Welcome, Mr. Emerson. Beans?

WALDO

Yes, Henry. Mrs. Emerson has sent me for
some beans.

Pause.

> HENRY

Beans.

> WALDO

Beans?

Henry nods. Waldo smiles. This is a game they play, a contest, and beneath the game the tension between them is only barely hidden.

Waldo thinks.

> WALDO

Pounding beans is good to the end of pounding empires one of these days.[26]

> HENRY

Ha!

Henry picks up a piece of paper and reads.

> HENRY

The same sun which ripens my beans illumines at once a system of earths like ours.[27]

Waldo nods.

---

[26] Emerson. *Eulogy of Thoreau*
[27] Thoreau, *Walden*

                    WALDO
You.

    Henry nods.

                    WALDO
Is that new?

                    HENRY
It is. A book I think. Maybe a lecture. But I
think it's a book.

                    WALDO
About?

                    HENRY
Me I suppose.

                    WALDO
You?

                    HENRY
Yes.

                    WALDO
You're writing about you?

                    HENRY
Franklin did it. Rousseau did it.

                    WALDO
Of course Henry. Of course.

HENRY

Even you have done it, Mr. Emerson.

WALDO

When?

HENRY

In your essay on Experience. You wrote about little Waldo. How you felt when he. Became ill. [28]

WALDO

Yes. Yes. But. That was to illustrate a point. I wasn't writing about myself.

HENRY

I am doing the same. Just on a slightly larger scale.

WALDO

What point are you illustrating?

HENRY

I'm not sure yet.

WALDO

I see.

HENRY

It's a work in progress.

---

[28] Emerson's son Waldo died of scarlet fever at age five.

WALDO

Aren't they all?

HENRY

It's about. My time here.

WALDO

DaVinci said that art is never finished.

HENRY

What I have learned.

WALDO

Art may never be finished, but that cannot be said for artists.

HENRY

What I have experienced.

WALDO

L'arte non è mai finita.

HENRY

What?

WALDO

DaVinci. That's what he said. I thought you knew Italian, Henry.

HENRY

Italian? A bit. I'm better at French. Latin. Spanish. German. Greek.

WALDO
And your English is coming along quite well too.

HENRY
Is it? Praise from Ralph Waldo Emerson himself. What more could one ask?

WALDO
You have so much promise Henry. I don't want you to waste it.

Henry holds up a sheaf of papers.

HENRY
I am transforming my journal into a book.

Waldo smiles.

WALDO
Now where did you learn to do that?

HENRY
I wonder.

Henry puts down the papers, looks around the cabin.

HENRY
I'm thinking of calling it Life in the Woods.

WALDO

These are hardly the woods, Henry.

Henry smiles.

HENRY

It is a domestic wilderness.

WALDO

Henry, you know I dislike it when you do that.
It is a rhetorical trick of which you are too
fond.

Henry smiles more broadly.

HENRY

I know.

Now Waldo smiles.

WALDO

Ha. Anyway, you're a mile from the town
common.

Henry pauses. Back to the game.

HENRY

Common.

Waldo takes his time. Then.

WALDO

Nothing astonishes men so much as common sense and plain dealing.[29]

Henry picks up his sheath of papers again.

HENRY

If one advances confidently in the direction of his dreams, and endeavors to live the life which he has imagined, he will meet with a success unexpected in common hours.[30]

They pause.

Waldo nods.

WALDO

You again.

HENRY

Yours was good though.

WALDO

Thank you. I'll have to try and remember it.

Waldo takes the sheath of papers from Henry.

---

[29] Emerson, *Art*
[30] Thoreau, *Walden*

He peruses them.

Mumbling.

Nodding.

Scowling.

Henry gets nervous.

HENRY
The town common is a mile and three
quarters.

WALDO
Not looking up
You are the surveyor. I bow to your superior
knowledge.
Now he looks up.
As to distance.

Henry smiles.

HENRY
You don't like the title Life in the Woods?

WALDO
Simple titles, Henry. One word if possible.
Nature. Experience. Self-Reliance.

HENRY
That's two words.

WALDO
It's hyphenated. Counts as one.

HENRY
I bow to your superior knowledge. As to
hyphens.

Waldo sits and glances around the cabin.

HENRY
Anyway, why are you working on something
new? I thought you were still reworking the
other one. The river book.

HENRY
A Week on the Concord and Merrimack
Rivers.

WALDO
Short titles, Henry. Short titles.

WALDO
I'll try to remember, Mr. Emerson.

WALDO
And three names. If you have them. Ralph
Waldo Emerson. David Henry Thoreau. It
adds gravity. We all need a little gravity.

HENRY
Henry David. I changed it.

WALDO

Really? Henry David Thoreau. Yes that sounds better. Perhaps I should have done that. Waldo Ralph Emerson?

Pause

BOTH

No.

WALDO

When you have Ralph and Waldo to choose from, I suppose it makes no difference.

HENRY

Emerson has a solid ring to it.

WALDO

Do you think?

HENRY

Oh yes.

WALDO

Perhaps. Perhaps you are just used to it.

HENRY

No one can pronounce Thoreau. They always put the accent on the second syllable.

WALDO

It is better to be infamously mispronounced than to be mispronounced infamous.

Henry pauses. Repeats the phrase to himself.

HENRY

That makes no sense.

Waldo pauses. Repeats the phrase to himself.

WALDO

True. It sounds good though.

HENRY

Fame is not something I shall ever know.

WALDO

It was not something I expected when I was a young minister in Boston. But here we are. Though some would say I am more infamous than famous.

HENRY

Ha.

WALDO

First the publication of my little Nature book, which caused so much ruckus. Then my Divinity School disaster.

HENRY

It was a fine speech.

WALDO

Lecture. Politicians give speeches.

HENRY

Sorry.

WALDO

They still won't allow me to speak at Harvard.

HENRY

Lecture. See I do listen.

Waldo laughs.

WALDO

Still.

HENRY

They don't know you.

WALDO

That is what fame is. Being widely unknown.

HENRY

That makes sense. I just can't quite figure out why.

WALDO

Fame.

Henry thinks.

HENRY

Rather than love, than money, than fame, give me truth.[31]

WALDO

All the toys that infatuate men, and which they play for,--houses, land, money, luxury, power, fame, are the selfsame thing, with a new gauze or two of illusion overlaid. [32]

They pause, thinking.

HENRY

You.

WALDO

I don't know. Yours has a power mine lacks, a straightforwardness. It reminds me of the way I used to write.

HENRY

A young man's phrase, you're saying. You think I will grow out of it?

WALDO

I hope not. I would write that way still if I could. If I still had that confidence. That clarity.

---

[31] Thoreau, *Walden*
[32] Emerson, *Fate*

Waldo picks up a paper on the desk.

WALDO
Your essay on Thomas Carlyle? It was
published?

HENRY
It was. Though Mr. Greely is having trouble
getting me paid for it.

WALDO
Lectures, Henry. That is what the public
wants. And you get paid in advance.

HENRY
You do.

WALDO
Your lecture on Thomas was well received.
Many of our friends remarked on it.

HENRY
I don't think lecturing is for me.

WALDO
Why not?

HENRY
I can't say what I think.

WALDO
Since when? I have never known you to hold
back your opinions. On anything.

Henry nods, and smiles.

HENRY
We have that in 'common'.

WALDO
I suppose we do.

HENRY
People don't like me.

WALDO
Everyone likes you Henry. It's just.

HENRY
Yes?

WALDO
They don't understand you. You read all these
languages, you are a fine poet, and the best
surveyor in Massachusetts, yet you made
pencils for a living.

HENRY
Those pencils were an excellent design. I made
many improvements. I will stack my pencils
up against any.

WALDO
You shouldn't be stacking pencils; you should
be using them. This is what I'm saying Henry.
Anything you do you do well. And yet what
you do is. Well. People don't understand it.

HENRY
I don't need them to.

WALDO
Like this, for example. Moving here. Building
your cabin. It makes no sense to anyone.

HENRY
Channing approves.

WALDO
Don't tell me you are taking advice from
William Ellery Channing.

HENRY
He has three names.

WALDO
Channing is simply happy he isn't the oddest
person in Concord anymore.

HENRY
Is that what I am?

WALDO
Yes, Henry. Yes, you are without doubt the
oddest person in a community of very odd
people. Channing. Bronson Alcott. His
daughter Louisa.

HENRY
Your Aunt Mary.

WALDO

I beg your pardon! Alright, yes. Though for
her I would prefer the term exceptional.

HENRY

I would agree.

WALDO

Hawthorne is very odd.

HENRY

Odd? Is that the right word for him?

WALDO

Peculiar?

HENRY

Uncanny?

WALDO

Bizarre?

HENRY

Curious?

WALDO

Weird?

They pause.

TOGETHER

Weird.

HENRY
He is from Salem. They are all weird there.

WALDO
His wife Sophia is from Salem also.

HENRY
Well. Perhaps not all.

WALDO
Another exceptional.

HENRY
Jones Very.

WALDO
He is not from here.

HENRY
He is of here.

WALDO
True. Poor Jones Very.

HENRY
Too much prophesy in his poetry.

WALDO
And yet the sanest mad man I ever met.

HENRY
Harvard will do that to you. Speaking of,
Willie Goodwin.

WALDO
You think? I have some hopes for him.

HENRY
And then of course there is you.

WALDO
Me? I am not odd.

HENRY
Ha!

WALDO
I am not. I am normal. I am average. I simply think and read and write more than other people.

HENRY
You think that is not odd?

WALDO
I am the opposite of odd. With me it is simply too much normal. Which is why I attract so many odd people. They find me, like opposite poles.

HENRY
Like the sun. We all gravitate around you, but never approach, lest we burn up in the fire of your mind.

WALDO
Hardly. It sounds good though.

HENRY
Is that why I came to you?

WALDO
I couldn't say. Could you?

Nelly bustles in, full of purpose.

NELLY
Papa, the Captain has asked if you would read
again after supper this evening.

WALDO
The captain? But.

He makes the mental transition. Slowly.
Nelly waits patiently.

WALDO
Again? Surely they do not wish to be bored
again.

NELLY
Everyone enjoyed it. And so did you.

WALDO
I suppose. It is more difficult now.

NELLY
I'll be there Papa. Right next to you.

WALDO
Daughter. You should be living your own life,
not fiddling away with your fumbling father.

NELLY

Papa this trip has been such a joy for me. How else could I have met the people we have met? Seen the places we have seen? London, Paris, Rome, Florence, and now Egypt. And to have you all to myself these months.

WALDO

We seem hardly ever to be by ourselves.

NELLY

Everyone wishes to see and be seen with the great Mr. Emerson. And to hear him. What will you read tonight?

WALDO

Must I?

NELLY

No. Of course not. I can explain to the captain.

WALDO

No. No. I will. I have earned my keep that way for fifty years. Why stop now? Perhaps he will refund our eight dollars.

NELLY

The passengers will be delighted.

WALDO

A bit of poetry perhaps?

NELLY

One of the short ones.

WALDO

Everything I write is short. I have a limited attention span.

NELLY

Oh yes.

WALDO

My longest work is only 90-some pages.

NELLY

Nature.

WALDO

Yes. Never had that stamina again. After that I realized it was easier to write short pieces and collect them. The Essays. English Traits. Representative Men. No one seems to have caught on yet.

NELLY

Well, you are a genius.

WALDO

And quotes. Always quote other writers. It lengthens the piece and it makes people think you know more than you do.

NELLY

So short works, lots of quotes. That's how you became the most world-famous American thinker since Benjamin Franklin.

WALDO

That. And your mother. If I had not found her, at the time. I don't know. I think my life would have been very different.

NELLY

At the very least, you would be on his journey with some other daughter.

Waldo laughs, sorts through the books on the desk, picks one up, turns the pages, reads.

WALDO

Give All to Love by Ralph Waldo Emerson. Three names. Very good.

Nelly looks at him, puzzled again.

WALDO

Give all to love;
Obey thy heart;
Friends, kindred, days,
Estate, good-fame,
Plans, credit and the Muse,—
Nothing refuse.

'T is a brave master;
Let it have scope:
Follow it utterly,
Hope beyond hope:
High and more high
It dives into noon,
With wing unspent,
Untold intent:
But it is a god,
Knows its own path
And the outlets of the sky.

It was never for the mean;
It requireth courage stout.
Souls above doubt,
Valor unbending,
It will reward,—
They shall return
More than they were,
And ever ascending.

Leave all for love;
Yet, hear me, yet,
One word more thy heart behoved,
One pulse more of firm endeavor,—
Keep thee to-day,
To-morrow, forever,
Free as an Arab
Of thy beloved.

Cling with life to the maid;
But when the surprise,
First vague shadow of surmise
Flits across her bosom young,
Of a joy apart from thee,
Free be she, fancy-free;
Nor thou detain her vesture's hem,
Nor the palest rose she flung
From her summer diadem.

Though thou loved her as thyself,
As a self of purer clay,
Though her parting dims the day,
Stealing grace from all alive;
Heartily know,
When half-gods go,
The gods arrive.

NELLY
That's lovely, but perhaps too short?

WALDO
No such thing.

NELLY
I think they might prefer one of your essays.

WALDO
One of the older ones perhaps. Self-Reliance.

He picks up another book, turns the

pages.

Nelly tries to interject but he goes ahead.

WALDO

I read the other day some verses written by an eminent painter which were original and not conventional. The soul always hears an admonition in such lines, let the subject be what it may. The sentiment they instill is of more value than any thought they may contain. To believe our own thought, to believe that what is true for you in your private heart is true for all men, -- that is genius. Speak your latent conviction, and it shall be the universal sense; for the inmost in due time becomes the outmost,--and our first thought, is rendered back to us by the trumpets of the Last Judgment. Familiar as the voice of the mind is to each, the highest merit we ascribe to Moses, Plato, and Milton is, that they set at naught books and traditions, and spoke not what men but what they thought. A man should learn to detect and watch that gleam of light which flashes across his mind from within, more than the lustre of the firmament of bards and sages. Yet he dismisses without notice his thought, because it is his. In every work of genius we recognize majesty. Great works of art have no more affecting lesson for us than this. They teach us to abide by our spontaneous impression with good-humored inflexibility then most when the whole cry of voices is on the other side. Else, to-morrow a stranger will say with masterly good sense precisely what we have thought and felt all the time, and we shall be forced to take with shame our own opinion from another.

He pauses.

WALDO
I like that one. It reminds me of who I used to think I could be.

NELLY
Papa, you read that one last night.

WALDO
I thought it sounded familiar. Too often these days my own words return as strangers.

He turns more pages.

WALDO
My essay on Experience?

NELLY
Oh Papa. Not that one.

WALDO

I am surprise that you remember it. You are
very young when it was published.

NELLY

I remember it. But.

*She looks through the other
books on the desk.*

How about one of the newer ones?

Waldo reads.

WALDO

Experience. By Ralph Waldo Emerson.

The lords of life, the lords of life,--[33]
I saw them pass,
In their own guise,
Like and unlike,
Portly and grim,
Use and Surprise,
Surface and Dream,
Succession swift, and spectral Wrong,
Temperament without a tongue,
And the inventor of the game
Omnipresent without name; --
Some to see, some to be guessed,
They marched from east to west:
Little man, least of all,

---

[33] Essay on Experience, Emerson – edited a bit

Among the legs of his guardians tall,
Walked about with puzzled look: --
Him by the hand dear nature took;
Dearest nature, strong and kind,
Whispered, `Darling, never mind!
Tomorrow they will wear another face,
The founder thou! these are thy race!'

Waldo acts as if he is at podium giving a lecture.

WALDO

Where do we find ourselves? In a series of which we do not know the extremes, and believe that it has none. We wake and find ourselves on a stair; there are stairs below us, which we seem to have ascended; there are stairs above us, many a one, which go upward and out of sight. But the Genius which, according to the old belief, stands at the door by which we enter, and gives us the lethe to drink, that we may tell no tales, mixed the cup too strongly, and we cannot shake off the lethargy now at noonday. Sleep lingers all our lifetime about our eyes, as night hovers all day in the boughs of the fir-tree. All things swim and glitter. Our life is not so much threatened as our perception. Ghostlike we glide through nature, and should not know our place again. Did our birth fall in some fit of indigence and frugality in nature, that she was so sparing of her fire and so liberal of her earth, that it appears to us that we lack the affirmative principle, and though we have health and reason, yet we have no superfluity of spirit for new creation? We have enough to live and bring the year about, but not an ounce to impart or to invest. Ah that our Genius were a little more of a genius! We are like millers on the lower levels of a stream, when the factories above them have exhausted the water. We too fancy that the upper people must have raised their dams.

Waldo starts to weaken, to fumble, to forget.

WALDO

If any of us knew what we were doing, or where we are going, then when we think we best know! We do not know today whether we are busy or idle. In times when we thought ourselves indolent, we have afterwards discovered, that much was accomplished, and much was begun in us. All our days are so unprofitable while they pass, that 'tis wonderful where or when we ever got anything of this which we call wisdom, poetry, virtue.

Nelly steadies his hands.

WALDO

Some heavenly days must have been
intercalated somewhere, like those that
Hermes won with dice of the Moon, that Osiris
might be born. It is said, all martyrdoms
looked mean when they were suffered. Every
ship is a romantic object, except that we sail
in. Embark, and the romance quits our vessel,
and hangs on every other sail in the horizon.
Our life looks trivial, and we shun to record it.
Men seem to have learned of the horizon the
art of perpetual retreating and reference.

Waldo loses his place. She points it out.

WALDO

How many individuals can we count in
society? how many actions? how many
opinions? So much of our time is preparation,
so much is routine, and so much retrospect,
that the pith of each man's genius contracts
itself to a very few hours.

Waldo gains strength again.

WALDO

The history of literature—take the net result of
Tiraboschi, Warton, or Schlegel,—is a sum of
very few ideas, and of very few original tales,
—all the rest being variation of these. So in this
great society wide lying around us, a critical

analysis would find very few spontaneous actions. It is almost all custom and gross sense. There are even few opinions, and these seem organic in the speakers, and do not disturb the—

Waldo falters.

HENRY
Whispering
Universal necessity.

WALDO
Universal necessity.

WALDO
What opium is instilled into all disaster! It shows formidable as we approach it, but there is at last no rough rasping friction, but the most slippery sliding surfaces. We fall soft on a thought. Ate Dea[34] is gentle.

Waldo stops. Nelly takes the book and reads. Lights up on Ellen.

NELLY
The only thing grief has taught me, is to know how shallow it is. That, like all the rest, plays about the surface, and never introduces me into the reality, for contact with which, we

---

[34] Ate is the Greek Goddess of Delusion.

would even pay the costly price of sons and lovers. Was it Boscovich who found out that bodies never come in contact? Well, souls never touch their objects. An innavigable sea washes with silent waves between us and the things we aim at and converse with.

She offers him the book, points to the passage.

ELLEN

Grief too will make us idealists. In the death of my son—

Waldo gathers, goes on.

WALDO

In the death of my son, now more than two years ago, I seem to have lost a beautiful estate, — no more. I cannot get it nearer to me. If tomorrow I should be informed of the bankruptcy of my principal debtors, the loss of my property would be a great inconvenience to me, perhaps, for many years; but it would leave me as it found me, — neither better nor worse. So is it with this calamity: it does not touch me: some thing which I fancied was a part of me, which could not be torn away without tearing me, nor enlarged without enriching me, falls off from me, and leaves no scar. It was caducous. I grieve that grief can

teach me nothing, nor carry me one step into
real nature.

He stops again.

HENRY
The Indian who was laid under a curse, that
the wind should not blow on him, nor water
flow to him, nor fire burn him, is a type of us
all. The dearest events are summer-rain, and
we the Para coats that shed every drop.
Nothing is left us now but death. We look to
that with a grim satisfaction, saying, there at
least is reality that will not dodge us.

ELLEN
Dream delivers us to dream, and there is no
end to illusion.

Waldo closes the book.

WALDO
Yes. Yes. One of the more recent ones then.
My essay on Memory?

Nelly comforts him, then exits.

HENRY
You never told me what you thought of it.

WALDO
Thought of what?

HENRY
My essay on Carlyle.

WALDO
Ah. Well done. I said so.

HENRY
Exactly. You shook my hand. You said I did
well. But you never said what you thought.

WALDO
That is unusual for me.

HENRY
One might even say odd.

Ellen laughs, then exits or lights down.

WALDO
Well, it is difficult for me to judge. You know
only the words. I know the man.

HENRY
Does that make a difference? It was his words I
was writing about.

WALDO
It is hard for me to be objective.

HENRY
Why?

WALDO
The man is a friend.

HENRY

You can't be objective because he is a friend?

WALDO

I don't think so.

HENRY

Are you objective with me?

WALDO

It is not the same.

HENRY

You have no trouble criticizing me. You and
Margaret Fuller made something of a sport of
it.

WALDO

The pieces you sent to the Dial, they, we,
wanted to help. We see so much promise in
you Henry.

HENRY

You keep saying that. Of course I know that,
Mr. Emerson. I am grateful to you, and to Miss
Fuller.

WALDO

We want to see the remarkable abilities we
know you possess reach fullness. Maturity.

HENRY

As do I. Why do you think I came out here?

WALDO
I haven't the slightest idea.

HENRY
Don't you?

WALDO
Why did you leave us Henry? Didn't you like staying with us?

HENRY
Of course I did. You know I did.

WALDO
I thought you did. Everything was in its right place. Everything worked.

HENRY
For you.

WALDO
But not for you?

HENRY
It was not my place. It was not my home. It was not my. Family.

WALDO
We all cared for you Henry. The children. Mrs. Emerson.

HENRY
I know. I.

*Henry stops. He is getting into dangerous
territory.*

HENRY
So? What did you think of my lecture?

WALDO
I wish you had left me out of it.

HENRY
How? How can I leave you out of anything?
You are Ralph Waldo Emerson.

WALDO
The man who is banished forever from
Harvard Divinity School.

HENRY
The American Plato.

WALDO
The man who is foolish enough to spend his
life writing and thinking. Usually in that order.

HENRY
The successor to Montaigne. The genius of
Concord.

Henry pauses. The game again.

HENRY
Genius.

WALDO
In every work of genius we recognize our own rejected thoughts.[35]

HENRY
You're quoting yourself.

WALDO
It's hard not to.

HENRY
It breaks the rules.

WALDO
Were there rules?

Henry stares.

WALDO
Fine.

Waldo stares back, discerning.

WALDO
At first glance he measured his companion, and, though insensible to some fine traits of culture, could very well report his weight and caliber. And this made the impression of

---

[35] Emerson, Self-Reliance

genius which his conversation sometimes
gave.[36]

HENRY

It takes a man of genius to travel in his own
country, in his native village; to make any
progress between his door and his gate.[37]

*Emerson shakes his head, tired of the
game.*

WALDO

I cannot judge.

HENRY

You cannot not. You are everywhere for me.
Except here. In this cabin.

WALDO

Except that I am here.

HENRY

But at least I am also here. I am myself here.
This is my place. This pond is my pond. These
beans are my beans. And I am finding my way
here. To something different.

WALDO

Different from me, you mean.

---

[36] Emerson, *Tribute* to Thoreau, Atlantic Magazine,
1862
[37] Thoreau, Journal 1851

> HENRY

There is only one Ralph Waldo Emerson.

Long pause.

> WALDO

How are the beans this year?

> HENRY

The late freeze took the crop. Until then I expected twelve bushels.

> WALDO

Fertilizer?

> HENRY

None. Except the mold left over from the stumps when I pulled them.

> WALDO

Economical.

> HENRY

Of necessity.

Waldo looks slyly at Henry.

> WALDO

Necessity.

Pause.

HENRY

The better part of the man is soon plowed into the soil for compost. By a seeming fate, commonly called necessity, they are employed, as it says in an old book, laying up treasures which moth and rust will corrupt and thieves break through and steal.[38]

WALDO

We are sure, that, though we know not how, necessity does comport with liberty, the individual with the world, my polarity with the spirit of the times.[39]

They pause.

HENRY

You.

Waldo nods.

WALDO

Henry.

HENRY

Of necessity.

Waldo walks around the cabin, inspecting.

---

[38] Thoreau, *Walden*
[39] Emerson, *Fate*

WALDO
The cabin is holding up well.

HENRY
You have not visited in a while, Mr. Emerson.

WALDO
I did not wish to disturb your work. You said you were making progress.

HENRY
I was. I am. I think.

Henry pauses.

WALDO
How much longer do you plan to stay?

HENRY
That is up to you.

WALDO
How do you mean?

HENRY
This is your land.

WALDO
Henry. Please. I don't wish to argue. At least not about that.

HENRY
We are who we are.

WALDO

I came here to tell you. I'm going away.

HENRY

West? South?

WALDO

East. Back to Europe.

HENRY

How long?

WALDO

Six months this time. Possibly longer.

Pause

HENRY

When?

WALDO

September.

HENRY

Impossible. What of your trees sir?

WALDO

My orchard you mean?

HENRY

You may possibly get in your peaches by then,
the Early Rose and the Presidents. And your
pears may well be fine, the Seckels and the
Bloodgoods certainly. But what of your apples?

The Gravensteins, the Bellflowers. and the
Hightops? And the quince. Don't get me
started on the quince.

WALDO
I do love quince apple pie. Mrs. Emerson's pies
are the wonder of New England.

HENRY
I remember.

WALDO
The orchard has never fared so well as when
you were tending it, Henry. So I thought. I was
hoping. We all, the family, you see, were
hoping.

HENRY
No.

WALDO
Your apple needs you Henry. The one we
named for you. The Thoreau is wasting away
in your absence.

HENRY
I have my work here.

WALDO
I don't understand this choice, Henry. When
you asked to build out here, I agreed. But I
didn't understand. I still don't.

HENRY

My work is here.

WALDO

You are a talented poet.

HENRY

I'm not a poet. I don't know what I am but it
isn't a poet.

WALDO

Then write something else.

HENRY

I'm trying.

WALDO

Solitude is necessary. I understand that. But
isolation? For one with your temperament. Is
that wise?

Henry pauses.

HENRY

Wisdom.

WALDO

Henry.

HENRY

Wisdom.

WALDO

Can't we?

HENRY

Wisdom.

WALDO

To finish the moment, to find the journey's end in every step of the road, to live the greatest number of good hours, is wisdom.[40]

HENRY

How insufficient is all wisdom without love[41].

Neither speaks for a moment.

WALDO

The children miss you Henry.

HENRY

I still see them.

WALDO

Mrs. Emerson misses you.

HENRY

I miss them all.

WALDO

Then come home, Henry.

---

[40] Emerson, *Experience*
[41] Thoreau, *Journals*

HENRY

It isn't my home. I will never have a home.
Not in that sense. Nor wife. Nor children. I
know that now. It is not a life meant for me.
Or a life I wasn't meant for.

WALDO

You don't have to make that choice. I know
there is a pressure. Yes there are
compromises. Money. Making a living. Home.
Wife. Children to care for. Interruptions
certainly. From the work we do. But they are
necessary. I don't know how to say it. I'm not
speaking of love.

HENRY

Don't, sir.

WALDO

A life together. A wife. A companion through.
Children. The things they teach you. The
foundation they give you.

HENRY

I saw that foundation crumble.

Waldo pauses, sinks into a chair.

HENRY

I loved him too.

WALDO
He was a beautiful child.

HENRY
I saw him suffer just as you did.

WALDO
My beautiful boy.

HENRY
I saw him die.

WALDO
My Waldo.

HENRY
The same year.

WALDO
I know.

HENRY
The same year.

WALDO
I'm sorry.

HENRY
The same year as John.

WALDO
Your brother was. We all.

HENRY
Waldo from scarlet fever and John from
tetanus.

WALDO
I have never left that room.

HENRY
Five years ago.

WALDO
Is it five?

HENRY
The year your essays were published. I don't
know how you managed it. I don't know.

WALDO
It's what we do.

HENRY
It is. Yes.

WALDO
It's what we must do.

HENRY
It's what I am doing.

WALDO
Necessity.

HENRY
Necessity.

WALDO
If so say so Henry. I don't understand, but I do trust.

HENRY
You see what you invite me back to.

WALDO
Dear boy. Can't you see that...

HENRY
No. It is not that way, with us. Don't romanticize it. That's not who we are.

WALDO
Are you sure?

HENRY
I have loved.

WALDO
It's not important.

HENRY
I have loved.

WALDO
Yes yes.

HENRY
I still love.

WALDO
Mrs. Emerson.

Henry turns quickly.

HENRY
Sir?

WALDO
Mrs. Emerson. She would.

HENRY
Yes.

WALDO
She wished me to ask.

HENRY
Yes.

WALDO
Mrs. Emerson would like some beans. If there are any left. That is what I came to ask.

HENRY
Really?

WALDO
She would take me to task if I forgot.

HENRY
For.

WALDO
You know Lidian.

HENRY
I know Mrs. Emerson.

Waldo walks slowly to the door. Stops.

WALDO
Henry?

HENRY
What I have, I'll bring.

WALDO
I know. It's what we do

Waldo starts to leave again.

WALDO
Henry.

HENRY
Yes, Mr. Emerson?

WALDO
I am not objective.

HENRY
Sir?

WALDO
About you. I am not objective about you.

Henry waits.

WALDO

I believe that I am less objective about you
than any friend I have ever had.

HENRY

Thank you, Mr. Emerson. I'll try to remember
that.

Lights fades on Henry. He exits.

WALDO

Do please, Mr. Thoreau.

Waldo looks around him.

WALDO

Good spot for a cabin. I hope it lasts.

Ellen laughs. He smiles at the sound.

WALDO

That is familiar.

Lights up on Ellen.

ELLEN

Shall I remind you?

WALDO

Yes. Remind me. Please. Re<u>mind</u> me.

ELLEN

We met on Christmas day. You were my
favorite gift. I was a woman of 16 and you

were a boy of 24. We spoke of Byron. You thought I meant the poet and I thought you meant my spaniel. We were very confused for a moment, and then then your stern and serious ministerial face crinkled up and you laughed and laughed. And I decided then and there that you would marry me.

WALDO
You had a dog named Byron. I thought that was funny.

ELLEN
That you remember! I would be insulted but he was a very good dog.

WALDO
Byron.

ELLEN
A year later you brought me a book called *Forget Me Not*. A year! Now that is funny.

WALDO
That is ironic. It's not the same.

ELLEN
What is ironic is that I grew up in Concord, New Hampshire, and after I died you settled in Concord, Massachusetts.

WALDO

That is not ironic. It is a coincidence, and
possibly a metaphor.

ELLEN

I wanted to be a poet and you wanted to be a
minister. You ended up a poet and I ended up
a memory. What is that?

WALDO

That is a tragedy.

ELLEN

Oh, your poetry is not that bad.

He looks at her.

WALDO

That is funny.

She curtseys.

ELLEN

Are they coming back?

WALDO

What?

ELLEN

The memories.

WALDO

Oh they come back occasionally. I just had a
long talk with. But. They don't stay.

ELLEN

Shall I?

WALDO

What?

ELLEN

Stay?

He looks offstage where Nelly has exited.

WALDO

Ellen is...out there.

ELLEN

I am Ellen.

WALDO

You are Ellinelli. You are Lady Frolick and Lady Pensero.

ELLEN

I believe so.

WALDO

I have remembered something that I have forgotten.

ELLEN

You had forgotten but now you remember?

WALDO

No, I remember that I have forgotten.

ELLEN

I see.

WALDO

I have tried and tried.

ELLEN

Yes?

WALDO

For some time, I have tried.

ELLEN

Yes?

WALDO

I cannot recall.

ELLEN

Say it.

WALDO

Your face. I cannot recall your face.

ELLEN

Is that all?

WALDO

I want to. Very much. But I cannot.

ELLEN

I'm almost glad. I was not so beautiful toward
the end. So pale and thin.

WALDO

You were always beautiful.

ELLEN

But wait. You have my miniature still?

WALDO

Your picture. Yes. I have it in my study. Or I did. Who knows where it is now? I don't think it burned. Though that night was so confusing.

ELLEN

Poor Waldo.

WALDO

That I remember. You called me that often.

ELLEN

If you have the miniature, then you can't have forgotten how I looked.

WALDO

I look at the painting. Often. But I do not recognize you when I see it.

ELLEN

Was it not a good likeness?

WALDO

It's not that. It just doesn't feel the same.

ELLEN

The same?

WALDO

As when I looked at you. I still remember the way I felt. Transcendent.

ELLEN

Transcendent? You make me sound very grand.

WALDO

You were.

ELLEN

Transcendent? No. I was a girl in love, for the first and only time. You mistake transcendent for incandescent.

Her lighting brightens a bit

WALDO

Transcendent sounds better.

ELLEN

You're just used to it[42].

WALDO

Perhaps.

---

[42] Emerson was the founder of American Transcendentalism.

ELLEN

I suppose I was a little transcendent, towards the end. It was so hard to hold on to life. I tried, for you.

WALDO

You were brave. I remember that.

ELLEN

We had so little time. I didn't want to waste it in tears.

WALDO

And your cough. Your terrible cough. And the blood. So much blood from such a tiny body.

ELLEN

I am healed now.

WALDO

I took you south, to try the climate.

ELLEN

To Philadelphia!

WALDO

And I had to leave you there and return to Boston. I have never felt so alone.

ELLEN

I was the one in Philadelphia.

WALDO

And I was desperate to know if you missed me
as much as I missed you.

ELLEN

That is natural. You were so young.

WALDO

Natural. You were young. Was I ever young?

ELLEN

You were. You just didn't know it.

WALDO

I feel younger now, with you here.

ELLEN

Dear Waldo.

WALDO

Dear Waldo. I remember that, now, too. No
one else has ever called me that. Lidian calls
me Mr. Emerson. May I speak of her to you?

ELLEN

Sweet Waldo.

WALDO

I know she has never called me that. Not in my
hearing anyway.

ELLEN

You love her.

WALDO

It is, imprecise, to use the same word for what
I felt for you, and what I feel for her. But it is
the only word we are given. Even Shakespeare
never found another. So I suppose we must
make do.

ELLEN

But this dream of love, though beautiful, is
only one scene in our play. In the procession
of the soul from within outward, it enlarges its
circles ever, like the pebble thrown into the
pond, or the light proceeding from an orb.[43]

WALDO

That sounds like something I once wrote.

ELLEN

It is.

WALDO

If you are a memory, how is it that you know
something I wrote years later.

ELLEN

Memories don't abide alone. We coexist.

WALDO

Really?

---

[43] *Essay on Love*, Emerson

ELLEN

Oh yes. We even speak to one another.

WALDO

Speak?

ELLEN

Yes. We speak often.

WALDO

Really. Memories speak to memories.

ELLEN

Well, think of it. What else is there to do but speak to each other? Especially when you spend so little time with us. Such a busy important man, always running around giving speeches.

WALDO

Lectures, not speeches. Politicians give speeches.

She sticks her tongue out at him through the veil, laughs, spinning away, her white dress flowing around her. She stops, then turns slyly back to Waldo.

ELLEN

I have had many conversations. With your brother Charles. With Henry Thoreau. In fact, Lidian and I have spoken.

WALDO

Pardon?

ELLEN

Lidian. Your second wife. You member her,
don't you?

WALDO

Oh yes.

ELLEN

I thought so. Lidian and I have had long
conversations.

WALDO

About me?

ELLEN

Oh yes!

WALDO

Oh no.

ELLEN

And she does call you poor Mr. Emerson, if
that is any consolation.

*Lidian enters, carrying stack of books on
top of which is a pie.*

He turns back to Ellen
For a memory, you are very chatty.

ELLEN

Memories are not miniatures.

WALDO

What are they? I don't remember.

ELLEN

Memory is a presumption of a possession of
the future. Now we are halves, we see the past
but not the future, but in that day will the
hemisphere complete itself and foresight be as
perfect as aftersight.[44]

WALDO

Or as imperfect. Did I write that?

ELLEN

Of course.

WALDO

It is like your face. Though I know it, I don't
recognize it.

ELLEN

I like that one especially. It reminds me of
your sermons. One of the saddest parts of
being sick was that I could not attend your
sermons.

---

[44] *Essay on Memory*, Emerson

WALDO

It reminds you?

ELLEN

You were so grand in the pulpit with your high cloak and sweet voice. And only once per sermon would you let yourself sneak a glance at your Ellinelli. And when you did look on my face, only for a second and with no smile or nod or sign, I knew I needed no other communion.

WALDO

Nor I.

He turns suddenly.

WALDO

I remember!

Ellen turns away.

ELLEN

My face?

WALDO

For a year afterwards, I walked each day to your grave.

He turns to her.

ELLEN

Poor Waldo.

WALDO
You asked me to.

ELLEN
Did I?

WALDO
Breathe not yet, but wait until
My spirit is set free.
Then whisper round my grave
The tale of my release —[45]

ELLEN
I wrote that.

WALDO
You did.

ELLEN
And you remember.

WALDO
I do.

ELLEN
But you cannot recall my face.

WALDO
No. I remember I walked each day to your
grave.

---

[45] *To the South Wind*, Ellen Emerson

He takes a step toward her.

WALDO
I needed to see your face. Once more.

Another step. Dimmer.

WALDO
Just once more.

Another step, and he is near her.

WALDO
One day I entered your tomb.

She turns to him.

WALDO
And opened the coffin.

He reaches up to her veil.

WALDO
And I saw.

Her light goes out. He lowers his arm.

WALDO
Nothing.

ELLEN
Nothing?

WALDO
Nothing.

ELLEN
It was empty?

WALDO
We were in darkness.

ELLEN
That is natural.

WALDO
Natural. Yes. Does it bother you?

ELLEN
What?

WALDO
That I, came to see you?

ELLEN
I come often to see you.

WALDO
Are you sure you are not a ghost?

ELLEN
Maybe a memory is a ghost that lives inside us.

WALDO
Maybe a ghost is a memory that lives outside us.

ELLEN

But you don't believe in the immortality of the soul.

WALDO

Maybe that is where memories go. The afterlife belongs not to us but to them.

She steps into the light again.

ELLEN

Perhaps they are us.

WALDO

After you died, I resigned from the ministry. I was lost, so I thought I may as well be lost somewhere new.

ELLEN

Clever Waldo.

WALDO

That's a new one. I wandered for a year. Syracuse. Naples. Rome. Florence. Paris. London.

ELLEN

So far from home.

WALDO

Without you I had no home.

ELLEN

So far then.

WALDO

I met great writers that I had admired: Landor,
Coleridge, Wordsworth, Carlyle.

ELLEN

Your Heroes.

WALDO

I found them to be...just men.

ELLEN

You were disappointed.

WALDO

Yes. But. It is a kind of freedom, to learn what
is possible, and by whom.

ELLEN

It is.

WALDO

By the end I knew something in me had
changed, but I did not know what.

ELLEN

I know.

WALDO

I came back, to Concord. I could not return to
Boston and the church.

ELLEN
I understand.

WALDO
I had to make a living, so I started writing, and speaking.

She smiles.

ELLEN
Lecturing.

And he smiles.

WALDO
Lecturing. I married Lidian.

ELLEN
A good woman.

WALDO
A good woman.

ELLEN
You needed her.

WALDO
I loved her. Love her. You can tell her I said so.

ELLEN
You can tell her.

WALDO

I can tell her.

ELLEN

She gave you children.

WALDO

Ellen. Edith. Edward. Poor Waldo, gone so young.

ELLEN

Poor Waldo. So much of tragedy.

WALDO

So much of life.

ELLEN

If I had not gotten sick...

WALDO

I could not have left you.

ELLEN

Maybe that is why I had to leave you.

WALDO

Let us build altars to the Beautiful Necessity.[46]

---

[46] *Essay on Experience*, Emerson

ELLEN

Though thou loved her as thyself,
As a self of purer clay,
Though her parting dims the day,
Stealing grace from all alive; [47]

WALDO

Heartily know,
When half-gods go,
The gods arrive. [17]

ELLEN

It's all right.

WALDO

I remember.

ELLEN

The loving. And the leaving. It is all right.

WALDO

Silent rushes the swift Lord
Through ruined systems still restored,
Broad-sowing, bleak and void to bless,
Plants with worlds the wilderness,
Waters with tears of ancient sorrow
Apples of Eden ripe to-morrow;
House and tenant go to ground.[48]

---

[47] *Give All to Love*, poem, Emerson
[48] *Threnody*, poem, Emerson

ELLEN

Lost in God.[18]

WALDO

In Godhead found.[18]

He returns to the desk.

WALDO

I have wondered from time to time what my
last memory will be. After all the others have
escaped me. What will be the last? Like
Pandora's box, my mind will shut tight, yet
one will tap on the lid and cry out "wait! I am
still here". Will it be you? Lidian? Nelly?
Henry? Little Waldo feverish in the bed? What
will it be? What part of myself will be the last
to say goodbye?

ELLEN

It may be a bit selfish but I should like it to be
me. But it won't be.

*She starts to exit as the light fades on
her.*

ELLEN

It won't be me. Or Lidian. Or Nelly. Or Henry.
Or little Waldo. For you it will be a boat on
river in a land where history waits.

WALDO

I have lived two lives. One of the mind. One of the heart. The mind is leaving. Only the heart remains.

He starts to exit.

WALDO

One monument to another.

The light slowly fades.

BLACKOUT

Epilogue (Optional)

Scene

Sleepy Hollow Cemetery, Concord, MA

Time:

January, 1883

Setting: An empty stage.

At Rise: Nelly is revealed, a book in her hand.

NELLY

The cast iron gates were flung wide, pearl-finished by a snow that had slowed finally to flurries. I took one step through the gates and even the sound of my breathing, so labored in the cold as I had walked up Lexington Road from our home, seemed swallowed by the frozen air. If this silence lasted an eternity, I thought, here was an audience that would appreciate.

The snow was wispy, dry. Barely half an inch powdered the road into the grounds of Sleepy Hollow Cemetery. Yet all colors had turned to white. The evergreen branches bowed under icy plumes. A slight breeze raised a miniature cyclone in front of me, guiding me, a lace-delicate spirit, that beckoned. I followed the white whorl.

No tracks disturbed the gleaming white path, which itself was barely distinguishable from the acres of alabaster waves. Regretting my footprints on the unstained way, I walked a few paces inward. The way wound left. I kept on straight. The high ground lay in the center. And here in the deep heart of Concord, my father lay at rest.

I soon found and climbed slippery steps to the flat of a hill. The path, dusted white under swaying trees, was marked on either side by stones. A ways down, I knelt in the snow. The marker had one word only: Henry.

Farther down, I passed our neighbors. Mr. Hawthorn on the left, the Alcotts on the right my old friend Louisa—died two days after her father Bronson— modest headstones all, though larger than Mr. Thoreau's.

The path turned right. I stepped in, one hand
on the massive stone we had placed. The brass
plaque embedded in the stone was partly
obscured by the snow, but I had no need of it,
for I knew his words well:

The passive master lent his hand
To the vast soul that o'er him planned

I stood looking down, having a curious urge to
speak to him. I wanted him to know that I did
not regret my choice, to care for him. That
knowing as I do now, as perhaps I did then,
that I will never marry, will have no children,
will live in our home in Concord until I die,
that I would have done the same. I wanted him
to know that the life he gave me, mind and
heart, was enough. But what do we know
when we are passed? Perhaps he knew. I do
not.

Yet I thought. Felt sure. That he would speak
to me. If anyone could. Whoever among us
knew more of eternity?

I waited. But after a few silent moments, I
turned and left, tracing my footprints carefully
in reverse as I stepped down, leaving
undisturbed whatever I could of the covering
under which they slept.

As I moved, some lines came to mind, all at once and complete. I repeated them over and over so I would not forget:

I looked for footprints, sure each step had shaped the earth, and found the earth enfolding them instead. As I left, I noticed my own footprints, nearly covered by wind and snow, but still enough to follow to the road. This was how they shaped the earth, I thought, with footprints just deep enough to point the way.

When I reached home, I went to his study, which we had left untouched since his death. I searched as I had done as a girl and found a book, his book, the one with all his heroes: Representative Men. I turned the pages until I found this passage:

She reads

All things are engaged in writing their history. The planet, the pebble, goes attended by its shadow. The rolling rock leaves its scratches on the mountain; the river its channel in the soil; the animal its bones in the stratum; the fern and leaf their modest epitaph in the coal. The falling drop makes its sculpture in the sand or the stone. Not a foot steps into the snow or along the ground, but prints, in characters more or less lasting, a map of its march.[49]

   BLACKOUT

---

[49] Emerson: Goethe; or, The Writer

STEPHEN EVANS

THE HISTORY

In July of 1872, Ralph Waldo Emerson's house in Concord, Massachusetts, caught fire. His many friends and admirers raised money for repairs, and to send him on a journey across the ocean while those repairs were being made. He was accompanied on the voyage by his daughter, Ellen Tucker Emerson, who was named for his first wife.

At the time of this voyage, Emerson was one the most famous Americans, and certainly the most famous intellectual since Franklin. Everywhere he went he was invited to speak and read from his works. But his mind, which had been declining for a few years, declined even more seriously after the fire. No longer considered capable of traveling alone, his daughter accompanied him and managed the trip.

This tale of a few moments on that voyage is imagined, though based in some details on the letters of Emerson's first wife Ellen and his namesake daughter Ellen, and his journals.

Emerson's journal for March 29, 1832, lists a quote from Aristotle and this cryptic single line:

I visited Ellen's tomb & opened the coffin.

BIBLIOGRAPHY

Plutarch:

The Morals, by Plutarch, corrected and revised by William W. Goodwin, Ph. D. 1870

Emerson Biographies:

(My favorites among many)

Emerson: The Mind on Fire by Robert D. Richardson Jr.

Ralph Waldo Emerson by Oliver Wendell Holmes Sr.

Emerson Correspondence:

Letters of Ellen Tucker Emerson, edited by Edith W. Gregg

Letters of Ralph Waldo Emerson, edited by Ralph L. Rusk

One First Love, The Letters of Ellen Luisa Tucker to Ralph Waldo Emerson, edited by Edith W. Gregg

Emerson Works:

Most of Emerson's own works are in print and/or available online.

Acknowledgements

The original version of *Monuments* opened as part of the play *Generations* on August 2, 2019, at Colonial Players in Annapolis, Maryland. The play was directed by Lois Evans and starred Jeffrey Miller and Kate Wheeler.

Generations also included the one-act plays *Last Laugh* by Morey Norkin and *Late Nights in Cars* by Michael Gilles.

STEPHEN EVANS

About the Playwright

Stephen Evans is a playwright and author.

Find him online at:

https://www.istephenevans.com/

https://www.facebook.com/iStephenEvans

https://twitter.com/iStephenEvans

https://www.gr8word.com

Books by
Stephen Evans

Fiction:

The Marriage of True Minds

Let Me Count the Ways (forthcoming)

The Island of Always

Two Short Novels

Painting Sunsets

The Mind of a Writer and other Fables

Non-Fiction:

A Transcendental Journey

Funny Thing Is: A Guide to Understanding Comedy

The Laughing String: Thoughts on Writing

Task of the Human-Hearted

Liebestraum

Plays:

The Ghost Writer

Spooky Action at a Distance

Tourists

Generations (with Morey Norkin and Michael Gilles)

The Visitation Trilogy (forthcoming)

Verse:

Limerosity

Sonets from the Chesapeke

STEPHEN EVANS

STEPHEN EVANS

CPSIA information can be obtained
at www.ICGtesting.com
Printed in the USA
LVHW032316250121
677442LV00006B/1046